THE VINDICATION OF JESUS CHRIST

A Brief Reader's Guide to Revelation

THIRD EDITION

James B. Jordan

Athanasius Press
205 Roselawn
Monroe, Louisiana 71201
http://www.athanasiuspress.org

The Vindication of Jesus Christ

Originally published by Transfiguration Press, Niceville, Florida.

10 09 08 3 4 5

ISBN: 978-0-9753914-8-8 (softcover)

Table of Contents

Table of Contents

Introduction

This survey of Revelation originally appeared in *Biblical Horizons* 101–106 (1998). It is a summary of a series of lectures on Revelation delivered over several years at Grace Presbyterian Church in Niceville, Florida. The tapes and study guides for these 204 lectures are available from Biblical Horizons. For several years Biblical Horizons also published a journal entitled *Studies in the Revelation,* which consisted of detailed studies in Revelation and related Biblical passages. Information on these and other studies available from Biblical Horizons can be found at the end of this volume.

Since this little book is only a survey, I obviously cannot argue in detail for every point along the way. The taped lectures and written material at the back of this book provide detailed arguments. My hope is that this survey will stimulate both pastors and laymen to read Revelation with new eyes, seeing that it is not as hard to understand as is usually imagined.

The second edition corrected typos and layout errors, with the result that pagination is somewhat different from the first edition. The third edition makes slight changes in phrasing here and there.

1
What Revelation Is About

Although Revelation is said to give a blessing to those who read it and hear it (1:3), it often results in confusion as well. Any reader is thrilled by the pictures of God's triumph over His enemies and His vindication of His saints, but as regards the specifics—well, who knows?

Revelation is applicable to all times and occasions in the Church, and because of that it has been interpreted as predicting many different events in history. Naturally, these interpretations all contradict one another, which leads many believers to decide that the book is a riddle wrapped in a mystery inside an enigma, and that efforts to understand it are a waste of time.

Not so. There is a very clear aspect of Revelation that tells us both when it was written and what it is directly concerned with. Once we understand this, we can understand the specific predictions in the book, as well as how the book continues to apply to every generation.

The clue is this: in the Book of Revelation, angels are portrayed as bringing final judgments on the creation. This tells us that the creation that is being judged is the First or Old Creation, and also tells us that the book was written before the final destruction of the Temple and Jerusalem in AD 70.

The word translated "angel" in the Bible means "messenger," and often refers to human beings. In Revelation 2 and 3, for instance, the "angels" of the churches are the pastors, those who bring God's message to their churches. For the rest, however, the messengers in Revelation are spirit angels.

Now the Bible tells us that the Old Creation was superintended by angels, while the New Creation is superintended by redeemed humanity. To save space, and because this essay is designed as a Bible study, I won't be writing out the passages. You must look them up yourself. Start with 1 Corinthians 6:3, which establishes that at the end of the New Creation we shall judge angels, not vice versa. Then, as regards the Old Creation consider Hebrews 2:2 and Acts 7:53. Turn next to Galatians 3:19, and then read Galatians 4:1–7. These passages show that in the Old Creation we were considered as children, and the angels were our tutors. The chief tutor originally was Lucifer, but he betrayed his calling in the Garden. So the Son of God entered as the Angel of the Lord to guide humanity toward maturity. Before He was the Second Adam, Jesus was the Second Lucifer. Throughout the Old Creation, we see the Angel of the Lord and His spirit angels supervising and judging humanity. Now, however, the man Christ Jesus has ascended to rule the angels, and in union with Him we also rule them.

What this means for Revelation is this: since angels are bringing the judgments, they must be judging the world that was committed to their charge. This cannot be the world of the New Creation; it must be the world of the Old Creation.

The New Creation began at Pentecost, when the ascended and enthroned Jesus sent the Spirit to enable us to disciple the nations and in that sense to rule the world. The Old Creation did not end at that time, however, because God gave the Jews and God-fearing Gentiles a period of time to make the transfer from the Old to the New. According to Matthew 23:34–38, all the sins and crimes of the Old Creation were to be rolled up and judged with the destruction of Jerusalem, which happened in AD 70. This was forty years after Pentecost.

God could not rightly judge the Old Creation simply for rejecting Jesus. The Law—His Law—requires the testimony of two witnesses. The second witness was the Holy Spirit. Jesus said that blasphemy against Him would be forgiven, but not blasphemy against (rejection of) the Holy Spirit (Luke 12:10; Acts 7:51; Acts 28:25–27). Many Jews and God-fearers did convert after the Spirit came, but for those who did not, wrath came upon them in the uttermost (1 Thessalonians 2:14–16).

During this period of overlap between the coming of the New Creation and the end of the Old Creation, Isaac and Ishmael were together in the house of God. Ishmael, however, was shortly to be cast out (Galatians 4:21–31).

Now, with these facts in mind, we can see that the period of time covered in Revelation is basically the same period of time covered in Acts and the Epistles, though it focuses on the final events of that period. This means that we can and should interpret Revelation in terms of what the rest of the New Testament writings have to say, and not speculate about later events. And naturally, connecting Revelation with Acts and the Epistles is going to make it much easier to interpret the symbols in the book.

The final destruction of the Old Creation is the public vindication of Jesus Christ. Repeatedly throughout His career, Jesus warned that destruction was going to come soon on the apostate Jews and on the whole old world. Occasionally He also predicted His own resurrection, but not nearly as often. Jesus' resurrection was a private vindication of who He was and what He did, but no one saw it take place, and Jesus only appeared to a few disciples. The destruction of the enemy city, Jerusalem, was His public vindication. Fulfilling Jesus' prophecies, it confirmed Him as a true Prophet, and as the last and greatest Prophet. It was the proof that He had indeed ascended to heaven and become King of kings and Lord of lords. Thus, the destruction of the Old Creation is of incalculable importance to Biblical theology. It was not some mere mopping-up operation, but was the great public historical vindication of Jesus by the Father. Those who fail to see this fact generally discount the importance of the destruction of Jerusalem, and thus fail to see why it occupies so much attention in the Gospels, and also fail to see that it is the major concern of the book of Revelation. We might just as well call Revelation "The Vindication of Jesus Christ." (At least one academic evangelical scholar has recognized this. N. T. Wright, *Jesus and the Victory of God*. Christian Origins and the Question of God, Volume 2 [Minneapolis: Fortress Press, 1996]. Though Wright does not deal with the book of Revelation, he demonstrates thoroughly from the Gospels that Jesus repeatedly predicted the destruction of Jerusalem as the event that would publicly vindicate His claims. Perhaps at long last the academics will begin to take up this important aspect of Biblical theology.)

Now, many Christians reject the idea that most of Revelation is concerned with the period from Pentecost to the end of the Old Creation in AD 70, because they think that this makes Revelation irrelevant for today's world. Not so, because the short history from AD 30–70 is a type or model for the long history of Christendom from Pentecost to the Second Coming. Because the events of Revelation are tied to the rest of the New Testament, we can identify for certain what Revelation is talking about, and that means we can make much better *applications* of Revelation to our own day, better than if we were merely speculating about what Revelation is talking about. Thus, the spirit-angels who blow the trumpets of God's Word in Revelation translate into Christian preachers and evangelists today. The beasts and seducers outside and inside the Church are still with us today.

2
The Author of Revelation

Liberal scholars, and too many evangelicals as well, start off by saying that "John" wrote Revelation, and then there is a discussion as to whether this "John" is the son of Zebedee or some other "John." Well, John wrote Revelation *down*, but the author of the book is plainly said to be Jesus Himself (1:1).

The Bible comes to us in three ways. First, many parts of the Bible were simply dictated by God (the Angel of the Lord) to men, who wrote down what they were told to write. This is true of parts of Exodus, almost all of Leviticus, much of Numbers, and most of the books of the Prophets (Isaiah, Jeremiah, etc.). Second, many parts were written under Divine inspiration, as God guided the thoughts of men who wrote under their own names or anonymously; books like Genesis, Judges, and the Psalms of David and Asaph. Third, some parts of the Bible were given to men in the form of visions, which they then wrote down under inspiration. Ezekiel 40–48, Zechariah 1–6, and the book of Revelation, for instance, were written this way. Revelation 2–3 was dictated to John by Jesus, of course.

Thus, we cannot expect Revelation to be written in the same style as the Gospel and Epistles of John. No doubt John the son of Zebedee was the human penman of Revelation, but it is not written in his style. Thus, there is no need to posit some other "John" as the author, someone with a different style.

3
The Language of Revelation

I am writing in English. The Book of Revelation is written in Symbol (1:1, "and He sent and symbolized it by His angel to His bondslave John"). Symbol is a language just as much as English or Russian is. And the fact that Revelation is written in Symbol is what makes it hard for those who don't know the Bible inside and out.

If you want to learn Russian, the first thing you must do is learn the Cyrillic alphabet. Then you learn the various words in Russian written in that alphabet. Shortly you can read very simple sentences made up of those words. After much study you can read Russian fluently. Finally you start to dream in Russian, and that is when you really know Russian.

The same is true of Symbol. The language Symbol starts in Genesis 1, which is a true account of the creation of the world, but which also gives us fundamental categories that are used in Symbol later on. The large Symbol passages are the second half of Exodus, all of Leviticus, much of Numbers, much of 1 Chronicles, and the books of Canticles, Ezekiel, Daniel, and Zechariah—as well as shorter parts of all the rest of the Bible.

We begin to learn Symbol by becoming familiar with the "words" in that language, words like "altar," "temple," "lampstand," "unclean," "blood," "clay pot," "bull, sheep, goat, pigeon, and dove," and the like. Then we see how those symbols are combined to form "sentences," like the rites of sacrifice in Leviticus, or the structure of and placement of furniture in the Tabernacle. Then we can see how these "sentences" form larger statements, whole essays written in symbols, such as the progression from Leviticus 10 to Leviticus 16, or the progression from Ezekiel 40 to Ezekiel 48. Finally we become so familiar with Symbol that we can live and move and have our being in it.

Now, the Bible is many things, and one of those things is a course in Symbol. Jesus, in Revelation, assumes that we know this language. He assumes that we are thoroughly acquainted with Leviticus and Ezekiel. We know which animals go with which sacrifices. We know and understand the rites of the sacrifices. We can walk around inside Solomon's Temple and explain it.

Because of this, someone like me can easily spend five years lecturing through Revelation, and can publish a quarterly journal devoted to it, while knowing that there are depths I have not yet begun to plumb. Because Revelation is written in Symbol, and because we twentieth-century Christians don't know this language at all, it takes us a lot of work to begin to understand the depths of Revelation.

As it happens, I have devoted many years to trying to learn Symbol. If you look in the Biblical Horizons catalogue, you will see not only my basic introductory book on this subject (*Through New Eyes: Developing a Biblical View of the World*), but also many particular studies. This has put me in a good position to understand Revelation. I cannot be so vain as to think I understand it completely, but in what follows I shall offer to you the fruits of my many years of inquiry.

Naturally, in this brief study I cannot plumb the depths of Revelation. And I shall be forced to assert many interpretations that I cannot take the space to argue and prove. This study is only an introductory one, and for more you will have to consult the more in-depth analysis available in the recorded lectures.

4
The Audience of Revelation

Revelation was not written to the Jews and Gentiles, but to the churches (1:4). This means it is written to us, we who live in the New Creation. Specifically, it was written to seven local churches in Asia Minor, positioned between Jerusalem and Rome and afflicted by both Roman persecutors and apostate Jews-Judaizers. (The Judaizers were those false Christians who sought to bring Gentile converts under the world of the angel-given law, as discussed in Galatians and elsewhere.) Let us build on the language of the apostle Paul and call these two groups (Jews and Judaizers) together the "Circumcision."

Each of these churches existed in a city, corresponding to the Temple in the city Jerusalem, and to Harlot-Jerusalem (the Circumcision) in the larger "city" of the Roman empire (the *oikumenē*, or commonwealth). Jesus writes to each of these churches, praising their good works and threatening judgments for their sins. Then He provides them, and us, with an object lesson: an eighth letter that concerns the judgments on the Circumcision and Rome. This eighth letter (the Seven-Sealed Book) is an object lesson to the seven New Creation churches, and thus is an object lesson to us as well.

Revelation is *not* concerned with the war between the Jews and the Romans, which resulted in the destruction of the Temple and Jerusalem. Rather, Revelation is concerned with evangelism, faithfulness, martyrdom, and the vindication of the saints who stand firm. It is addressed to churches, because the Church is the center of any culture in which she exists—whether she realizes it or not and whether that culture believes it or not. Judgment is the first step toward renewal and blessing, and such judgment starts at the house of God. When God's people are faithful, He makes their enemies to be at peace with them, by either converting or destroying their enemies.

Throughout the book of Acts the enemy of God's people consists of the Jews and Judaizers. These are considered one group in Revelation, which we are calling the Circumcision. They are called false apostles, Balaamites, Nicolaitans, the synagogue of Satan, and Babylon the Great Whore. In Acts, we routinely see the Romans defending the Church. Revelation predicts, however, that in the near future Rome, the "Beast," will also turn against the Church. Revelation extends the history in the book of Acts down to the end of the Old Creation.

5
The Literary Structure of Revelation

The reason the language Symbol exists is to say things that cannot readily be said in discourse languages. A symbol can indicate several things at once, if it exists in several symbol packages. For instance, the Tabernacle and Temple simultaneously symbolize the cosmos, the house of God, the social community, the individual human being, and the Messiah as perfect Man. Similarly, the altar is simultaneously a miniature holy mountain, God's people as a whole, the human person, and Jesus.

In the same way, symbolic narratives exist at more than one level. Think of Revelation as a polyphonic musical composition, in which several melodies are moving simultaneously but with perfect harmony and interaction. For instance, the book of Revelation follows the order of the festival year laid out in Leviticus 23, which in turn is based on the seven days of creation:

Sabbath—Light (Day of Lord)—Rev. 1
Passover—Establishment of Firmament People—Rev. 2–3
Firstfruits—Plants—Rev. 4–5
Pentecost—Lights—the Book, Rev. 6–7 (The Law was given on Pentecost.)
Trumpets—Summoning swarms of people to God—Rev. 8–15
Bowls—Man—Day of Atonement, Rev. 16–19
Booths—Great Sabbath—Rev. 20–22

Now, it would take too long for us to survey Revelation in terms of this symbolism, so we shall use another outline that is also found in the book. This outline is much more "on the surface" than the festival outline.

1. Prelude to the Seven Churches, ch. 1
2. The Seven Churches, ch. 2–3
3. Prelude to the Sealed Book, ch. 4–5
4. The Sealed Book, ch. 6–7
5. The Trumpets, ch. 8–12
6. Postlude to the Trumpets, ch. 13–15
7. The Bowls, ch. 16
8. Postlude to the Bowls, ch. 17–22

This structure is chiastic, which means it moves inward and back outward thematically, and moves from the glorified Jesus to the glorified Bride:

1. Jesus descends to earth to meet John
   2. The Seven Churches
      3. Jesus ascends to heaven
         4. The Seven Seals
         5. The Seven Trumpets
      6. The Church ascends to heaven (ch. 12–15)
   7. The Seven Bowls
8. The Church descends to earth (ch. 21)

Third, the book of Revelation as a whole is structured chiastically (see next page).

Each of these outlines is a way to read Revelation, and a way to read it correctly. As we shall see in a moment, there are other ways to structure the sequence of events in Revelation also. If you are using this essay as it is intended, as a study guide, take the time to read over Revelation in terms of each of these outlines, drinking in as much as possible of the structure and flow.

A. John and Jesus, 1

B. Churches, 2–3

C. Throne/s in Heaven, 4–5

D. Horses, 6:1–8 (first four seals)

E. Saints Under Altar, 6:9–11 (5th seal)

F. Judgment Starts, 6:12–17 (6th seal)

G. Saints Sealed on Earth, 7

H. Seven Trumpets Appear, 8:1–2

I. Pentecostal Era Begins, 8:3–5

J. Plants, 8:7

K. Gentiles, 8:8–9

L. Drink, 8:10–11

M. Heavens, 8:11–12

N. Army of Lies, 9:1–11

O. Army of Saints, 9:12–11:6

P. Massacre, 11:7–13

Q. Dragon, 12

Q' Sea Beast, 13:1–10

P' Massacre, 13:15

O' Army of Saints, 14:1–3

N' Army that does not lie, 14:4–5

M' Heavens, 14:6–7

L' Drink, 14:8

K' Gentiles, 14:9–13

J' Plants, 14:14–16

I' Pentecostal Era Ends, 14:18

H' Seven Bowls Appear, 15:1

G' Saints in Heaven, 15:2–4

F' Judgment Restarts, 15:5–18:24

E' Saints in Heaven, 19:1–10

D' Horses, 19:11–21

C' Throne/s in Heaven, 20

B' Church, 21:1–22:5

A' John and Jesus, 22:6–21

6
Fundamental Symbols in Revelation

Before we turn to a reading of the book, there is one other preliminary matter to get out of the way, which will save us time as we go, and that is to identify certain fundamental symbols that have confused many people. These are:

The earth. "Earth" is better translated "land," because it refers to the people associated with the Holy Land, the Circumcision. After the destruction of the Circumcision, "earth" means all humanity (ch. 21–22).

The sea. As the land refers to the Circumcision, so the sea refers to the Gentile world. This symbolism comes from Genesis 2, where the lands outside of Eden are watered by rivers. (Compare the symbolism of the book of Jonah; 2 Samuel 22:4–5; Psalm 65:7–8; Isaiah 5:30; 17:12–13; 57:20; Jeremiah 6:23; Ezekiel 27:25–36; Daniel 7:2–3.)

Mankind. In Revelation, "men" means the Circumcision. When Gentiles are spoken of, Revelation uses a four-fold list, usually "tongues, tribes, nations, and peoples," or some variant. Again, in chapters 21–22, "men" means human beings more generally. This four-fold list speaks of four types of civilization, in order:

Tongues—Patriarchal age, after the tongues of Babel.

Tribes—Mosaic age, when Israel and the Gentiles lived as tribes.

Nations—Kingdom age, when Israel and the Gentiles lived as nations.

Peoples—Oikumenical age, after Nebuchadnezzar, when Israel and the Gentiles lived as peoples within a large empire.

Buying and selling. Economic transactions in Revelation symbolize liturgical transactions. This is established in 3:18 (and compare 21:6). When those who refuse the mark of the Beast are not allowed to buy and sell, it means that they are expelled from the synagogue and Temple. The merchants of the land in Revelation 18 are those who worshipped at the Temple and synagogue. (Compare the moneychangers at the Temple, the repeated threats of expulsion from the synagogue and Temple in the Gospels, Acts, and the Epistles.).

Kings. Kings are those who rule over kingdoms. As regards the Gentile Beast, the kings are political rulers; but as regards the Jewish Land, the "kings of the land" are religious leaders (17:2, 18; 18:3, 8). God had given a preliminary kingdom to the Jews, calling on them to serve the nations. The rulers of that kingdom are not political leaders but religious ones: the scribes, Pharisees, and priests.

We shall glance at other symbols as we go, though of course we cannot in this survey deal with all of them. For a much more elaborate treatment of Revelation's symbolism, see my monographs *Behind the Scenes: Orientation in the Book of Revelation* and *The Revelation of Jesus in Revelation 1:12b–16 and its Relation to the Structure of the Book of Revelation*, both available from Biblical Horizons. With these things in mind, let us turn to a reading of the book itself.

7
Jesus: the Standard of Measurement
(1:9–20)

Repeatedly Revelation tells that the time of its fulfillment is near at hand (1:3; 22:10). All the "earth" will see (perceive, understand) Jesus "coming with the clouds" (1:7). "Coming with the clouds" never refers to a coming to the earth, but to an ascension, as it alludes to Daniel 7:13. Revelation shows us how Jesus began His Kingdom at His ascension.

John tells us that he was "in Spirit on the Lord's Day" (1:10). The sphere of the Spirit is the sphere of worship, when the Spirit-gathered assembly comes together in the Spirit before God on the weekly Day of the Lord. The whole book of Revelation takes place in and as a worship service. There is a call (ch. 1), an examination of sins (ch. 2–3), a declaration of the Kingdom and forgiveness (ch. 4–5), the reading of the Scripture (the Book and Trumpets), preaching based on the reading (10:8–11), a sharing of sacrament (the Bowls and Marriage Supper), and a call to go forth and take the gospel out (the River of chapter 22, and the call of the Spirit and Bride, 22:17).

Revelation is concerned with liturgical warfare. It is the prayers and the faithfulness of the saints before God's eye that set in motion the events in the book. The same is true today.

Jesus appears in Revelation 1:12–20. He is the Standard by which the churches are measured, and by which Babylon and the Beast will be measured also. He is described as having seven characteristics in 1:14–16, and if we list these, we see that they form a chiasm. These seven characteristics will be used to measure the seven churches, and also provide an outline of the book of Revelation as a whole:

Head—ch. 1, Jesus
  Eyes— ch. 2–3, evaluate churches
    Feet—ch. 4–5, are fit to go to the Throne
      Voice—ch. 6–7, the Book
    Hand—ch. 8–15, upholds the Church in tribulation
  Mouth—ch. 16–19, judges enemies (19:15)
Face-sun—ch. 20–22, glorification of Church

8
The Seven Churches Threatened
(2–3)

The symbols used for the seven churches are taken from seven periods of Old Creation history:

2:7 (Eden)
  2:10 (Joseph)
    2:14 (Wilderness)
      2:20 (Kingdom)
    3:2 (Judgment & Exile)
  3:7 (Restoration)
3:16 (Apostasy in Jesus' Day)

As you read the seven letters, ask yourself which church yours is most like. You will find particular help in these particular periods of Bible history.

Moreover, the seven letters anticipate Revelation as a whole. The enemy of the Seven Churches are the Nicolaitans (literally "people-conquerors," Judaizers), the false apostles pictured in Ephesus (2:6). The Jews-Judaizers of Smyrna take the main focus in chapters 6–12. The Beast and False Prophet (Balak and Balaam—literally "people-eater") are in chapter 13 and Pergamum. The Harlot Jezebel (ch. 17) is in Thyatira. The judgment on Jerusalem (ch. 18) is threatened against Sardis. The conquering army of saints (ch. 19) is pictured in Philadelphia. The choice whether or not to enter the New Jerusalem is set before Laodicea (3:20).

The seven letters are arranged chiastically. Ephesus and Laodicea have fallen into laxity. Smyrna and Philadelphia are both faithful, but one is small and persecuted, while the other is powerful and effective—an important lesson: faithfulness does not automatically mean either prosperity or persecution. The three middle churches are in a kind of progression. Pergamum has a few wicked people, who must be cast out. In Thyatira, the wicked are about as strong as the righteous, and a full war is needed. In Sardis, the wicked outnumber the righteous. The message is clear: if Pergamum does not resolve its evils, it will become like Thyatira; and if it does not deal with matters then, it will become like Sardis.

Jesus has one overall message to all the churches: you need to kick some people out!

The message is that church discipline must be exercised, and exercised without qualms, or else Jesus Himself will come and do it—and that is *not* a desirable outcome!

Having issued these warnings, Jesus then proceeds to show the churches just what it will mean if He has to come and purge their sins. It will mean the kinds of things found in the Seven-Sealed Book, the eighth letter to the eighth church: Babylon.

9

The Ascension of Jesus

(4–5)

In chapters 4 and 5 we are first shown God the Father on His throne. He is surrounded by an emerald rainbow, and the emerald is the stone of Levi. These Levites, however, are twenty-four archangels, the heavenly model of the twenty-four groups of Chief Levites and Chief Priests who served in the Temple according to 1 Chronicles 24–25. Closer in are the four cherubim, who lead in the heavenly liturgy.

We are told in 4:10 that the twenty-four archangels will fall down and worship God and cast their crowns before Him. This forecasts the drama of Revelation, for we shall find exactly twenty-four actions by archangels in the book. Each archangel in his turn comes before the Throne, removes his crown of ruling the Old Creation, and then goes forth to perform his last act of judgment against that

Creation. This pile of crowns is then picked up by the saints, who enter heaven to replace the archangels as co-rulers with Jesus (20:4).

The first archangel comes forward with a sealed book. This is the book of the Kingdom, which has been sealed up heretofore. All creation laments that the Kingdom has not really arrived, because there is no Adam worthy to take the Book and rule from it. Then Jesus appears, in the form of a slain lamb, having paid the price for our sins, and is found worthy. He is given the book, and all creation rejoices. While formerly they chanted their praise of God, now they take up instruments and sing.

The Book is really a large scroll. It is sealed along the edge with seven large wax seals, and it is implied that on each seal is embossed a picture. These are the things that kept the Kingdom from coming, that kept the Book from being opened. Jesus will break the seals, thereby releasing the grip of the Old Adamic Creation. Then He will proceed to proclaim what the Book says in the Trumpets and implement it in the Bowls of judgment. Thus, the rest of Revelation down to 22:5 is the contents of the Book, the eighth letter, the letter that warns the seven churches of what will befall them if they don't shape up.

The Twenty-Four Archangels

A. One Strong Angel (5:2)
  B. Seven Trumpet Angels (ch. 8–11)
    C. Four Leading Angels (9:14–15; also 7:1–2)
    C' Four Judging Angels (14:8, 9, 15, and 17+19)
  B' Seven Bowl Angels (ch. 15–16)
A' One Strong Angel (18:21)

The Bowl Angels include:

a. The prophetic angel (1:1; 17:1, 7; 21:9; 22:6, 8, 16)
b. The water angel (16:5)
c. The solar angel (19:17)

10
Releasing the Kingdom
(6:1–8:5)

There are those who say that the Seals, Trumpets, and Bowls each cover the same ground, each recapitulating the same events. This is not the case, as we shall see. The Seals open the Book. The Trumpets are the proclamation of the contents of the Book. The Bowls are the application of those contents. Historically, the Seals concern the very beginning of the Kingdom in AD 30. The Trumpets concern the events from Pentecost to the end of that period, just before AD 70. The Bowls concern the events of the end. Of course, the Kingdom has the same characteristics at its beginning, middle, and (first) ending, so that there are lots of parallels between the Seals, Trumpets, and Bowls. But the notion of recapitulation completely destroys the clear order of presentation in the book of Revelation, which is progressive, not cyclical.

Let us now consider the Seals, bearing in mind that breaking the Seals releases the Kingdom at last.

The first four Seals liberate four horses and four riders, called by the four cherubim.

> Lion calls White Horse of Evangelical Conquest
>
> Ox calls Red Horse of Interpersonal Conflict
>
> Man calls Black Horse of Sacramental Power
>
> Eagle calls Green Horse of Final Judgment

The four horses are the Church, and the four riders are Jesus. See Zechariah 2:6 and 6:1–5, which show that horses are the Church, which is governed by Jesus. The colors of the horses come from the colored stones of the tribes of Israel.

The sequence of the horses is the sequence of evangelism and conquest. First comes the Word of God, proclaiming Jesus as King. White is the color of Naphtali, the tribe that symbolizes the Bride. Next comes conflict, the Red Horse. Red is the color of Judah, the tribe that led in war. This is *not* a picture of political warfare, but of the kind of conflict Jesus predicted, as mother turns against daughter, and brother fights brother. It is the conflict experienced in every society when the Gospel comes, and it is the conflict experienced by the Jewish and Gentile believers in the period Revelation specifically deals with.

The third horse, the black, seems to have to do with famine, but this is not an economic famine of ordinary food. The three foods mentioned are the sacramental foods of the Bible: grain, wine, and oil (James 5:14). Bread is alpha food, what you eat in the morning; wine is omega food, what you drink when your work is done. Bread is priestly; wine is kingly. Bread focuses on the Old Creation, when men were priests but not yet fully kings (since Jesus had not yet ascended); while wine focuses on the New Creation, when we rule in sabbath rest with Jesus. Moses brought manna; Jesus made wine. The Black Horse pictures the gradual starvation of the old order, while the gifts of the new order are protected and preserved. Compare 7:3.

Black is the color of Joseph, the true baker and cupbearer (Genesis 40; 41:48–48; 44:2, 5). More accurately, Joseph's stone is the onyx, which is striped black and white, dark and light, for wine and bread. Here the horse is black because the horse is the new wine-church, and this wine is protected.

The Green Horse is the Levite horse, and we must recall that the Levites were the guards of the Tabernacle and Temple, armed with spears to kill anyone who approached the altar or sanctuary improperly. I believe that this horse brings actual physical conflict, the outbreak of a final violent conflict between those clinging to the old order and those converted to the new. This is what happened in the late AD 60s in Jewry, and it happens each time the Kingdom comes to a new people.

This is the sequence of events that brings the Kingdom to every nation of the world, fulfilling the Great Commission. It did not happen before AD 30 because the Kingdom was sealed up; but now it begins, and it will continue until Jesus returns at the end of history.

When the fifth seal is broken we see saints under the altar. This is the altar of incense, which represents the ladder from the firmament heavens to the highest heaven. The Holy Place in the sanctuary signifies the firmament heavens, while the Holy of Holies signifies the highest heaven, and the incense altar is right "below" that highest heaven. This is symbolically the place where the Old Creation saints went when they died. Because Jesus had not ascended to the highest heaven, they could

could not either. They waited in "Abraham's Bosom," "Paradise," until that day came.

Now the seal that restrained their full ascension has been broken and they expect to ascend with Jesus to the throne of God. Surprisingly, however, they are told that they must wait a little longer. They will not ascend until after a final harvest of martyrs, a final harvest of the Old Creation. This final group of witness/martyrs is sealed and set aside in chapter 7, and is martyred in chapter 14. Then they and all the Old Creation saints are avenged in the destruction of Babylon in chapters 17 and 18. After that, they all ascend to the throne to join Jesus in chapter 20 (compare Hebrews 11:40).

The sixth seal breaks the restraint on the final judgment of the Old Creation. Immediately the Old Creation starts to come to an end: the land quakes apart, the stars fall, the moon displays the blood of the saints before God's heavenly eye, and all men run to hide from the wrath of the Lamb. But as soon as this judgment starts, it is suspended, in mid-air so to speak. The judgment hangs over men, but is frozen in time until something else can happen. Just as the Old Creation saints must wait a little while, so must the final judgment on the Old Creation. That judgment will resume when we get to the Bowls in chapter 16. Meantime, the

Old Creation peoples are given a final opportunity to repent and be saved.

Chapter 7 continues with the sixth seal, explaining why the judgment is stopped. Four of the archangels come forward to seal a group of people on their foreheads (Genesis 3:19; Exodus 28:36; Ezekiel 9:4). The sealed people consist of a symbolic 144,000 converted Jews, symbolically 12,000 from each tribe except apostate Dan (Judges 17–18). These faithful Jews will be massacred by the apostate Circumcision in Revelation 14.

The third vision within the sixth seal shows a vast multitude of Gentile believers, who are also going to be massacred in the great tribulation that is about to come in the late AD 60s. These are the Christians killed by Nero and his representatives in the Roman Empire, the Beast. They are shown before God's throne, because that is where they are going to go when they die (14:13).

A numbered host of Israelites and a vast "mixed multitude" of converted and unconverted God-fearing Gentiles made the exodus from Egypt. The same is now taking place in the exodus from the Old Creation to the New. Revelation takes place in the forty-year "wilderness" period between AD 30 and AD 70.

When the seventh seal is broken, the singing in heaven stops for half an hour. It takes up again when this period of history is over, after the martyrdom of the saints, in chapter 15. The singing stops so that the trumpets can be heard. Liturgically speaking, the praise stops for the sermon to be heard.

The seventh seal held back the Holy Spirit, who is now poured out as fire. The fire poured out in 8:5 is *not* a picture of wrath as such. Rather, the reference is to the tongues of fire that came from the Spirit in Acts 2 (compare Daniel 7:10 and Revelation 4:5). The Spirit is poured out by "Another Angel." This Angel is not one of the twenty-four, but is their Captain, the Angel of the Lord, the Son of God.

Now the scroll is open, and the proclamation can begin.

11
Trumpets of Warning
(8:6–11:18)

We now see seven more of the twenty-four archangels step forward. Each has a word to proclaim, a trumpet to blow. These are warnings, because in each case only a third of things are destroyed. Many of these are like the warning plagues that God sent upon Egypt before destroying their firstborn and army.

The first trumpet sounds against the land, the Circumcision.

The second trumpet sounds against the sea, the Gentiles.

The third trumpet sounds against the springs of water, which refers to the Temple (Genesis 2:10–14; Ezekiel 47). The bitter waters are the poisonous doctrine that flows from the corrupted Temple, in contrast to the laver of cleansing water that God had put there. Here also we find the first of the seven names of Satan in Revelation: Wormwood, a poisonous plant. Satan takes his seat in the Temple because the Circumcision rejected Jesus. With him on this seat is the High Priest, the Man of Sin of 2 Thessalonians 2, the Land Beast and False Prophet of Revelation.

The fourth trumpet sounds against the sun, moon, and stars. Notice that this fourth trumpet connects to the fourth day of creation, and in the light of this we can connect the others to the other days. The heavenly bodies symbolize rulers and governors (Genesis 1:4–18). Jesus is now King, and all other rulers must fall before Him.

The last three trumpets are said to be woes against the land, against the Circumcision. We are still in the book of Acts, when the Romans still protected the Church against the Circumcision.

The fifth trumpet releases Satan and his swarming demonic army of the Circumcision from the pit of hell. Preaching salvation by law and works, they torment men (the Circumcision) for five months, the period of time between Pentecost and the Feast of Trumpets. Their evil doctrine does not torment the elect, however, who know that they are justified by faith alone. Satan is given two more names: Abaddon and Apollyon.

The sixth trumpet, like the sixth seal, contains three visions. Each of these is a vision of the Church. An army of 200,000,000 angels rides the horses of the Church to do battle with the enemy, and to "kill" men by converting them, putting their flesh to death with the fire of the Spirit breathed from their lion-of-Judah mouths.

(Let me add that these two visions have nothing to do with Roman campaigns against the Jews in the AD 60s. It is the Spiritual warfare of the Church against the world that is in view.)

The second vision of the sixth trumpet shows us John himself as a member of this army. He is called to preach part of the Book, a small book taken from the larger one. This small book is delivered to him by the "Other Angel," Jesus Himself. The content of this small book is the Seven Thunders, which John starts to write down, but is told not to. Instead, the seven thunders will be revealed as "Great Voice" events in the ensuing parts of Revelation.

The third vision of the sixth trumpet concerns the two witnesses, which are a symbol of the 144,000 faithful who proclaim the Word of God to Jewry. They are Spirit-empowered (olive-oil fed) lampstands in the dark world, imagery taken from Zechariah 4. They are like Elijah and Moses (11:5–6). They form a testimony of two witnesses against Jewry, like the two angels who visited Sodom, like Moses and Aaron in Egypt (11:8). Because of the power of their witness, the Beast from the Abyss (9:1–11) is driven back for a while to the pit, but eventually he comes out again and they are killed (17:8).

Their bodies lie "in the street of the Great City, which spiritually is called Sodom and Egypt, where also their Lord was crucified" (11:8). After Jezebel in 2:20, this is the second allusion to Babylon. What is Babylon? It is the original city-and-tower that tried to be a false religious center to reach to heaven (Genesis 11). She is a harlot, a false bride and daughter. These facts tell us that Babylon is certainly *not* Rome or any secular power. Rather, she is the false church, as most pre-modern expositors of Revelation understood quite well. Most pointedly, Babylon is Jerusalem, but by extension, she is the Circumcision throughout the Roman *oikumenē*, tentacles of Jerusalem. As Babel was a city with a tower, so Jerusalem is a city with a tower, the Temple, that "reaches to heaven."

The wicked Circumcision are happy that the witnesses are dead. They send presents to each other, as the Godly Jews did after the death of their enemies in Esther 9:19. The Gentiles, however, reflect on the death of the witnesses, and many convert (11:13).

This event, the massacre of the witnesses, corresponds to the massacre of the 144,000 in Revelation 14. As we shall see in a moment, the "postlude" to the Trumpets, chapters 12–15, review this same period of history from another angle.

When the seventh trumpet sounds, all creation praises God that the kingdom of Jesus has become manifested and will endure forever. The last event of the Old Creation is over, and all that remains is for the Bowls of wrath to clean up the mess.

12
The History of the Trumpet Times
(11:19–15:4)

The seven trumpets lay out themes or characteristics of the period between Pentecost and the final judgment of the Old Creation. The postlude to the trumpets, chapters 12–15, lays out the history of that period symbolically, displaying the spiritual realities and conflicts that operate behind the scenes in Acts and the Epistles, and in what follows the end of Acts.

We begin with the incarnation and ascension of Jesus, the seed of the woman. Satan tried to prevent Jesus from coming into the world: seducing Cain to murder Abel, trying to corrupt Israel in Egypt, seeking to destroy the Davidic line through Athaliah, and moving Herod to try and kill the baby Jesus. He failed, and Jesus went to heaven, where, as Michael the Arch-archangel, he cast out Satan. (The last four names of Satan are given here: Dragon, Serpent, Devil, Satan.) Satan was cast down to the land, where he took up residence in the Temple as Wormwood—but only for a short time.

Right away he sought to persecute the woman, the bride of Christ. These are the events of Acts 3–7, ending with the stoning of Stephen. The woman fled into the wilderness, which we see in Acts 8 as the saints flee Jerusalem. After a number of years of peace for the Church (Acts 9:31), Wormwood poured out his poisonous waters, false Judaizing doctrines, to try and corrupt the woman. God raised up Paul to defeat Satan and the Judaizers, and meanwhile the land (the Circumcision) drank up his false doctrine.

Satan has engaged in two tactics: persecution and corruption. These have failed. So now he decides to return to persecution, but this time against the non-Jewish believers, the "rest of her offspring." He stands on the sands of the sea, addressing the Roman Gentile sea, and raises up the Sea Beast.

The Beast comes from Daniel 7. God set up the original Sea Beast(s) as guardians and protectors of His people, four earthly cherubim-guardians. There were four Beasts, with seven heads among them; ultimately one Beast. Each time a Beast went bad and turned against God's people, God would remove it and bring in a new Beast. Thus, Nebuchadnezzar and his successor favored the Jews, but when Belshazzar mocked God, God raised up Cyrus. When the Persians stopped protecting the Jews, God brought in Alexander. And so forth. These are the Beasts and heads:

Beast 1	Head 1	Babylon
Beast 2	Head 2	Persia
Beast 3	Head 3	Alexander of Greece
Beast 3	Head 4	Greek Egypt (King of the South, Daniel 11)
Beast 3	Head 5	Greek Syria (King of the North, Daniel 11)
Beast 3	Head 6	Hellenistic Rome
Beast 4	Head 7	Imperial Rome

We have to remember that Rome was essentially a Greek city-state. The language of the Roman empire was Greek. The New Testament is written in Greek. The line of emperors corrupted the original Roman order, and eventually took it over. In the book of Acts we are still in Hellenistic Rome, and Rome protects the Church. When Nero came to the throne, he began to change Rome in earnest. The city burned down in AD 64, and Nero blamed the Christians. This was the end of old Rome and the full arrival of new Rome, the seventh head, the fourth beast. That is the event that Satan brings to pass in Revelation 13. It is the death wound from which Rome recovers. It is the killing of the sixth head, and the coming of the seventh.

Thus the Guardian Beast goes bad for the last time, and attacks the faithful among the Gentiles (13:7). Meanwhile, the Circumcision worship him. Now, if you had asked any Jew if he worshipped Caesar, he would likely have struck you dead for asking! But in fact, when they had a choice they said, "We have no king but Caesar." In their heart of hearts, they rejected Jesus and worshipped power, which means that they worshipped Caesar. They wanted a political kingdom, not an ethical-spiritual one; they wanted a Jewish Empire to replace the Roman Empire. (Remember when you read Revelation 13 that "earth" means "land," the Circumcision.) Revelation is dealing with the spiritual realities behind the scenes of history, and the reality was that the Circumcision worshipped Caesar, even though they also hated him.

Then we have a second Beast, a Land Beast. This is clearly a Jewish (land) Beast, also called the False Prophet (and the Man of Lawlessness of 2 Thessalonians 2). He has two horns, and copies the Sea Beast. The two horns are the Herods and the High Priests. It is a fact that the Herods were the semitic (Edomite) servants of Rome in Palestine, and also a fact that the

Herods appointed the High Priests.

Now, in 13:14, we find that the False Prophet/Land Beast calls down fire from heaven to the land. While this partly points back to Elijah at Mount Carmel, as a counterfeit thereof, in context it is a false Pentecost, a counterfeit of 8:5. It is also, very importantly, a counterfeit of the fire that God sent upon the altar when the Tabernacle and Temple were finished (Leviticus 9:24; 2 Chronicles 7:1). The Pentecostal fire of Acts 2 was a sign that Jesus had constituted His new Temple, the Church.

What event is pointed to in 13:14? I believe it is the completion of Herod's Temple, the evil counterfeit Temple that enshrined not the shekinah glory of God but Wormwood. The Temple was completed in AD 64, the same year that Rome burned and new Rome began to be built. The completion of the Temple was taken as a sign by the wicked Circumcision that God was on their side. It encouraged them to rebel against Rome, which resulted in their destruction. But it also encouraged them to persecute the Christians as never before. Now they were finally absolutely certain that the Christians were wicked apostates who should be put to death according to the law of God in Deuteronomy 13. The completion of the Temple resulted in a false Pentecost of enthusiasm, and consequently the persecution and martyrdom of believers, of the two witnesses, of the 144,000.

The False Prophet sets up an Image for the Sea Beast, and orders that those who do not worship the Beast Image are to be killed. Worshipping the Beast Image is signified as buying and selling, and requires the mark of the Beast on hand or forehead. The Beast Image is the completed Temple. Just as the true Temple is an outward symbol of the kingdom of the God who dwells within it, so the false Temple is an outward image of the kingdom of Wormwood, who dwells within it.

We should note that this false worship is called image worship. True worship in Revelation is associated with the Book and the Small Book, and with faithfulness "to the Word of God and to the testimony of Jesus." False worship is worship with images. The history of the Christian Church shows that the temptation to fall into the service of images, in violation of the second commandment, is an ongoing problem.

Finally, the number of the Beast. It is said to be the number of man, a human number. As always, "man" means "Jew." It is a Jewish number. It comes from 1 Kings 10:14, which begins the section of Kings dealing with the fall of Solomon into sin. The law of Deuteronomy 17 forbad the king to multiply gold, women, and horses, but here we see Solomon do all three. In Revelation, the religious rulers of the "land" are called kings, the "kings of the land." The apostasy of the High Priest, and of the religious leaders of Israel, is thus linked to Solomon's sin. As Solomon lost his kingdom when the northern tribes rebelled after his death, so the Land Beast will lose his kingdom permanently when Jerusalem is destroyed.

Note: 666 does *not* have anything to do with Nero Caesar. It is a Jewish number, and refers to the religious leaders, the false Solomons, of Jewry. The Sea Beast is a counterfeit of God the Father and the False Prophet of God the Son. As the Son is the Word and Number of the Father, so the (Jewish) Land Beast is the name and number of the Sea Beast. The Sea Beast is Gentile; his number is Jewish.

Finally, we should note that the three great enemies in the Bible are the apostate (Genesis 3), the murderous brother (Genesis 4), and the seducing foreign woman (Genesis 6). These become Jewish apostate religious leaders, Edomite murderers (descendants of brother Esau), and Gentiles. Jesus was put on trial by the Jewish Sanhedrin, the Edomite (Idumean) Herod, and the Roman Pilate. Paul was tried by the same three groups. I mention this because it is usually overlooked that the Herods are part of the Biblical prophecy. Here the Sea

Beast is the Gentile enemy, the Land Beast is primarily the Herodian enemy, with the High Priest as his ally, and the Beast Image is the Jewish enemy.

In chapter 14 we have a picture of the great massacre commanded by the Land Beast. In 14:1, the 144,000 are on the earth with Jesus on Mount Zion, but in 15:2, they are in heaven. In the meantime they have been martyred. This company of people is identified as the firstfruit harvest of the New Creation (14:4), and they simultaneously complete the harvest of the Old Creation.

Six angels appear in this chapter. Four are from the twenty-four archangels, while two are the Angel of the Lord, the "Other Angel":

1. Jesus as Angel, 14:6
2. Archangel, 14:8
3. Archangel, 14:9
4. Jesus as Man, 14:14
5. Archangel, 14:15
6. Archangel, 14:17
7. Jesus as Angel, 14:18 (8:1–5)

First Jesus preaches gospel, good news, to Jews and Gentiles. The good news is that the hour of judgment has come. That hour will start with the great tribulation, the massacre of the saints. It will continue with the destruction of Babylon, and will end with the destruction of Beast and False Prophet.

(Note: The great tribulation is *not* the suffering of the Jews in the investiture and destruction of Jerusalem, but the suffering and martyrdom of the saints at the hands of the Circumcision and Gentiles.)

Following Jesus, an archangel declares that Babylon is fallen, amplifying the judgment Jesus has just pronounced.

Then another archangel declares that those who apostatized from the Church and compromised with the evil Temple would be cast into hell. Note that hell is said to be right before the throne of God. Sinners hate God worse than anything, and the greatest punishment for sinners is to be forced to endure His presence forever. Verse 12 says that this awful warning is designed to help the saints persevere in the tribulation. Their suffering will cause them to be tempted to go with the Circumcision, but this fearful warning will help them persevere.

In verse 13 we are told that those who die in the Lord from now on will be blessed. That is, no longer will they have to go to Abraham's Bosom and wait for heaven to be opened. This final martyrdom will lead to the opening of heaven's doors, and all the saints will go in, as we see in 15:2.

At the center of the seven persons in chapter 14 appears the Son of Man, who stands ready to reap the grain harvest. An archangel comes out and exhorts Him to do so. He puts in His sickle, and the harvest is reaped.

Then another archangel appears with a sickle to reap the grapes. Jesus, the Other Angel of 8:1–5, calls on him to reap the grapes, and he does so.

Now, bread and wine are symbols of the body and blood of Christ, and not only of Jesus individually but also of His whole body, the Church. Jesus plus the Church is called in theology *Christus Totus,* the Whole Christ. The harvest of grain and grape is the harvest of this sacramental army, the final massacre of the martyrs.

The reason some are tempted to say that the grape harvest is a harvest of the wicked is that the grapes are thrown into the great wine press of the wrath of God. This statement does not mean that the grapes are pressed by the wrath of God. It means that the wine produced by the grapes carries the wrath of God. This is quite clear in what follows: the blood of the grapes completely covers and fills the land. Now, in the Bible, blood cries out for vengeance. The blood covering the land cries out for God's vengeance. The blood cries for God's wrath, and that is what follows immediately in the outpouring of the Bowls. The blood is the blood of the saints, which is avenged by God's wrath. (Genesis 4:10; Exodus 1:22 + 7:20 + 12:23; Numbers 35:9–34; Deuteronomy 21:1–9).

The grapes are trampled outside the city. This is another proof that the saints are in view, as they join Jesus outside the city in His death. Compare Hebrews 13:11–14.

This final massacre is what seals Babylon's doom.

Now, back in 6:6 we saw that there was a starvation of bread but a protection of wine and oil, signifying the starvation of the Old Creation and the protection of the New. Possibly, then, the harvest of the grain represents the judgment against the wicked Circumcision, while the harvest of the grapes represents the martyrdom of the saints. But the fact that the "wicked grain" is harvested prior to the "righteous grapes" reverses the historical order of these events in Revelation: first the tribulation upon the saints, and then judgment of Harlot and Beasts. Thus, I believe that both grain and grapes represent the Church.

In 15:1 the third great sign appears (12:1, 3): seven more archangels with the seven last plagues. These are the plagues that strike in response to the massacre of the saints. The saints, meanwhile, have moved from Abraham's Bosom to the highest heavens and stand on the sea of ice/glass before the door of the heavenly sanctuary, praising God. (This is the sea raised up above the firmament heavens in Genesis 1:6–8; cf. Exodus 24:10; Ezekiel 1:22; Revelation 4:6.) The saints have not yet entered the sanctuary, however.

13
Bowls of Final Judgment
(15:5–16:21)

The Bowls section begins in 15:5. Again we see the seven archangels come out. The full wrath of God is given to them in bowls by the four cherubim. Then the glory of God fills the heavenly palace and no one is able to enter it. At this point, all twenty-four archangels have left and their thrones are empty, but the saints have not yet entered to take the thrones. (The last archangel acts in 18:21, but he must have left his throne before this event, perhaps along with the seven bowl angels.)

Like the Trumpets, the first four Bowls are against the Circumcision, Gentiles, Temple, and Rulers. The focus is on the Circumcision, as the Bowls are poured into the land (16:1), but the judgment of Babylon is simultaneously a judgment on the whole Old Creation, for Babel was the fountain and center thereof.

Like the Trumpets, the seven Bowls give us seven characteristics of this final judgment, while the postlude (ch. 17–22; 17:1; 21:9) provides an historical narration of the actual events in symbolic form.

The first Bowl is against "men," those apostate Jews and Judaizers who worshipped the Caesar principle of power and politics instead of submitting to King Jesus.

The second Bowl is against the sea and completely kills the sea. The Gentile world ceases to exist. Gentiles only exist in contrast to the chosen priestly nation (Hebrews–Israelites–Jews). The Church is the new chosen people, the new priestly nation. With the elimination of the old chosen people in AD 70, the designation of everyone else as "Gentiles" ceased to have any meaning. While people who are racially and culturally Jewish and Greek and Roman continued to exist after AD 70, these people no longer had the particular callings they had in the Old Creation. The Roman Empire was no longer a special Guardian Beast, and the Jews were no longer a special priestly nation. After AD 70, all that remain are believers and unbelievers.

The third Bowl is against the Temple and its poisonous waters. In case we have missed the point, 16:6 reiterates that these judgments come as God's avenging of His saints, as punishment for every martyr from Abel to the 144,000 (Matthew 23:35). The altar saints, who asked "How long?" in 6:10, now say "Amen!" in 16:7.

The fourth Bowl concerns rulers and governors. The sun is not put out, but instead is magnified and becomes oppressive. Oppressive government is a punishment from God, and the reference here is to the increasingly oppressive Roman government over the Jews. But the Jews ("men") did not repent.

The fifth Bowl shifts from the Circumcision to the Beast. I believe this alludes to the chaos in Rome in the last years of Nero and in the chaotic "year of three emperors" (AD 68–69). Notice that here it is not "men" who blaspheme and won't repent, but "they," Gentiles.

The sixth Bowl sets up the Battle of Har-Magedon. In Hebrew, "Har" means "Mountain," and "Maged" means "Festival Assembly." The Battle of the Mountain of Festival Assembly is a battle at Mount Sinai, at Mount Zion, at the Church. The actual battle is pictured in Revelation 19, where, at the Festival Marriage Supper of the Lamb, a battle is fought in which the Beast is destroyed. We are to remember the battle against Amalek at the foot of Mount Sinai (Exodus 17).

Two armies are brought together. The first is the Army of the Kings from the Sunrising.

This is the army of the saints, whose Captain is the Angel of the Sunrising, Jesus Christ (7:2). The Euphrates is dried up so that they can enter the holy land.

The second army is the Three Frog Army. The three frogs are counterfeits of the Holy Spirit, proceeding from the counterfeit God (Dragon), Father (Sea Beast), and Son (False Prophet). They gather the leaders of the Roman *oikumenē* to fight the Church. Chapter 17 gives us more information about this. Spiritually speaking, Satan gathered the wicked Romans together with the wicked Circumcision to fight the Kingdom, but the Romans decided to destroy Jerusalem instead (17:3, 7, 14, 16). Then, at the Battle of the Mountain of Festival Assembly, Jesus and His people destroyed the Beast (19:19).

Then the seventh Bowl is poured out, and the events of 6:12–17 are allowed to resume. The judgment that was suspended 40 years earlier is now completed. Both Babylon and the realm of the Gentiles fall, and only the City of God remains. Once again let us remind ourselves that Revelation is telling us of the true spiritual realities that lie behind the appearances of history. Human cities still remain on the earth, and so do wicked governments. The Roman empire did not cease to exist in AD 70. But as a spiritual power energized by the full power of Satan in his Old Creation strength, all these human empires fell and ceased to exist.

14
The Judgment of Babylon
(17–18)

While Babylon is centrally Jerusalem, the symbol embraces more than just the city. As the center of the priestly people of the Old Creation, Babylon-Jerusalem extends to the whole holy land and to the Circumcision wherever they are. Harlot Babylon sits on many waters, perched on the watery sea of the nations (17:1, 15). Simultaneously she sits on the Beast, the symbol of the God-established but Satan-perverted guardian. These two symbols counterfeit the throne of God, for just as the Beast seeks to be God, and the False Prophet seeks to be God, so also Babylon seeks to be God. (Indeed, this is the reason these powers eventually turn against each other.) God is enthroned on the flood above the waters (Genesis 1:2; Psalm 29:2, 10). God sits enthroned above the heavenly guardians, the cherubim (above the Ark of the Covenant, and in Ezekiel 1).

The Harlot is also in a wilderness. When we last saw the Godly woman of the Church, she was in the wilderness (12:14), under assault by the evil Judaizing doctrines. The fact that the Whore is pictured in the wilderness tells me that she is not only the unbelieving Jews, but also the Judaizers, the counterfeit Church. She is the Circumcision as a whole. The Harlot displays the Israelites who died in the wilderness after leaving Egypt. They were delivered, but rejected the deliverance. Meanwhile, the faithful entered the Promised Land, as does the Bride in Revelation.

On the forehead of the High Priest was written on a golden flower, "Holy to Yahweh." The Harlot as counterfeit High Priest has on her forehead, "Babylon the Great, Mother of Harlots and of the Abominations of the Land"—not Yahweh but His apostate Bride claiming to be God; not holy but abominable.

The Whore is drunk with the blood of the saints. Previously the blood of the saints spread over the land had called down the vengeance of God. Now we see that the apostates have that blood inside themselves, as a kind of anti-sacrament, calling down judgment into their innermost parts (Numbers 5:11–31).

The Beast on which the woman sits is a

combination of the Red Dragon (Satan) and the Sea Beast (Rome, which propped her up through its agents, the Herods). The more ultimate power is, of course, the Dragon, the Beast of the Abyss (9:1, 2, 11). This Abyss Beast "was," when he led the Circumcision against the Church in 9:1–11 and 12:15. Then he "was not," when he was defeated by Paul and the Apostles. Shortly he is to come back out of the abyss for his final attack on the Apostolic Church, seen in 11:7 and 13:15–17. Eventually he will go to destruction. First, his Sea Beast and False Prophet agents will be destroyed (19:20), and then Satan himself (20:10).

This statement dates the book of Revelation. It was written before the attack in AD 64 by Nero in Rome and by the Circumcision when the Temple was completed in Palestine. It was written after Paul had definitively defeated the Judaizers, an event that we can date at the end of Acts, around AD 60–62. (The Spirit's victory over the Judaizers was definitive but not total, as there are still "false apostles" and "Balaamites" [people eaters] and "Nicolaitans" [people conquerors] in the seven churches of Revelation 2–3.)

More symbols are given in 17:9. The seven heads are also seven mountains, the Beast-kingdoms on which the woman sits. (These are *not* the seven little hills of Rome, nor some supposed seven hills of Jerusalem.) The mountains/heads exist in sequence, as kings, the personification and heads of their empires. Five have fallen (Babylon, Persia, Alexander, Greek Egypt, and Greek Syria). One exists at present (Hellenistic Rome, still protecting the Church). One is about to come (Demonic Imperial Rome, in AD 64).

The seventh head is also an eighth. The explanation for this is in Daniel 7. The Little Horn is a head on the seventh head. He uproots three of the ten horns, which as we shall see are the ten Roman Emperors. He is the Herods, who were the face of Rome in Palestine, and had the full power of three Roman Emperors for part of that time. Three Roman Emperors gave their power to three Herods:

Augustus: to Herod the Great, who tried to kill Jesus.

Tiberius: to Herod Antipas, who killed John and Jesus.

Claudius: to Herod Agrippa I, who killed James.

The ten horns are ten kings. They are all on the seventh head, because Imperial Rome was on the rise for a century before it emerged victorious over Hellenistic Rome in AD 64. In each case, the new Beast-head was on the rise before it conquered and replaced the old Beast-head. The emperors were:

Julius Caesar	
Augustus Caesar	
Tiberius Caesar	
Gaius (Caligula) Caesar	
Claudius Caesar	
Nero Caesar	End of Julio-Claudian Line
Galba	Chaotic Year of the
Otho	Three Emperors
Vitellius	
Vespasian	Rewarded for punishing Jerusalem

Vespasian came to the throne in AD 69, and the Sea Beast ended in AD 70: no more Jerusalem to protect as Beast meant Rome was no longer a Guardian Beast.

(For more details on the Daniel background, see my *The Handwriting on the Wall: A Commentary on the Book of Daniel*, published by American Vision, Powder Springs, Georgia.)

These ten horns, considered collectively as the one Imperial Beast power, turn against the Harlot. Formerly the Romans had supported the Jews by granting them special privileges in the empire. Indeed, this is why they protected the Church early on, for they regarded it as a Jewish sect. When the Jews rebelled as a nation, after the false Pentecost of AD 64, Rome turned against them.

In chapter 18 we are given a picture of rejoicing and lamentation over the destruction of Jerusalem-Babylon. God's people are told to leave her (compare Matthew 24:15ff.). Then the three lamentations are predicted.

The first is the lamentation of the kings of the land, the religious leaders.

The second is the lamentation of the merchants of the land, the ordinary worshippers. The cargoes that are listed correspond to the items gathered to build the Tabernacle and Temple (Exodus 25:4–7; 1 Chronicles 28–29). The buying and selling connected with these cargoes relates back to 13:17, and has to do with worship transactions.

The third lamentation is that of Gentile "seafarers" who had supported the Jews. These are those proselytes to Judaism who rejected the Kingdom. A four-fold list of them is given (18:17b), like the list "tribes, tongues, nations, peoples" found elsewhere.

Finally, the saints are called upon to rejoice in the prophecy of the destruction of Babylon.

In verse 21, the last of the twenty-four archangels dramatically hurls a stone into the water, signifying in part the scattering of the Jews among the Gentiles. The summary verse 24 explains once again that all this happened because the Husband acted to avenge His murdered Bride.

15
The Battle of Har-Magedon
(19)

In chapter 19 we see the rejoicing of the saints, who are now in heaven with the Father. It is time for the Great Festival of History to begin in earnest. The Great Festival began, of course, at Pentecost, but arrives in its fullness now that Ishmael has been cast out of the house of Abraham. As that Marriage Supper of the Lamb goes on, the Battle of the Mountain (*Har*) of Festival Assembly (*Maged*) takes place. The Church rides forth into history anew, following the now-vindicated Jesus to conquer all nations. The conquest of Jewry was only the first and definitive act in the Great Commission ("to the Jew first"). Now all nations are to be conquered by the Gospel, beginning with the Sea Beast and False Prophet. The nations are slain with the sword from Jesus' mouth, which is the preaching of the Kingdom.

The remnant of the kings of the land who survived the destruction of Babylon, as well as the Sea Beast and False Prophet (Herods and High Priests), are destroyed and removed from history.

16
The Millenium
(20)

After these events, in AD 70, the Millennium begins. A study of Biblical chronology will show that from the time of the building of Solomon's Temple to AD 70 is one thousand years. This was the first Millennium, the shadow of the greater Millennium. The literal foreshadows the figurative; the symbol of a Millennium arises from the actual thousand years of the first kingdom. (Note that Solomon's 666 apostasy is a foreshadowing of the 666 apostasy that ends that thousand-year first kingdom.)

(The first thousand years are as follows:

403 years from Temple to exile
70 years of Babylonian exile
490 years from Cyrus to 3½ years after the Crucifixion
37 to AD 70

This involves taking the seventy weeks of Daniel 9 literally for computational purposes.)

At the beginning of the Millennium, Satan is cast back into the Abyss. This does not mean Satan can do nothing, but that he can no longer deceive the nations and keep the Kingdom from them. He cannot do what he did in 13:1. He is bound from deceiving all the nations fully and simultaneously.

Meanwhile the ascended saints move into the Palace-Temple of God, and sit on the thrones vacated by the archangels, there to rule with Christ (20:4a). This heavenly rule is not for a "millennium," but is forever.

At the same time (20:4b–6), the Church on earth experiences a resurrection. In a sense, our personal salvation is a first resurrection, as we move from death to life. Baptism is also considered a first resurrection. In Revelation 20, though, it is the corporate restoration of the Bride after AD 70 that is called the first resurrection. (Compare Ezekiel 37 for the use of bodily resurrection as a symbol of national restoration.)

The rest of the dead do not rise until the Last Day. In view of Revelation 14:13, I believe that Christians go to reign with Christ in heaven when they die, joining the enthroned saints. The "rest of the dead" thus are the wicked, who are given back their bodies at the

Last Day, only to be cast into the lake of fire before the throne of God.

Verse 7 tells us that the Millennium, which began 40 years after Jesus' ascension, will not last all the way to His second coming. There is a brief period of time after the Millennium in which Satan will once again be released from the Abyss. Once again he will deceive the nations, Gog and Magog (prince and people; Ezekiel 38–39), to attack the Church. This final assault will be cut short by fire from heaven and the Last Judgment.

When God fills His Temple, no one can remain in it, as we have seen. At the Last Judgment, God will come and fill all of heaven and earth, and they will "flee away." Then all men will be judged and rewarded according to their faith-full or faith-less deeds.

A final note. When Satan is loosed it is so that he can deceive *all* the nations of the four corners of the earth (20:8). Clearly Satan is loosed to deceive particular nations at particular times, when God sees that such a judgment is needed. Nazi Germany and Soviet Russia stand as good examples of formerly Christian nations that were brought under such deceptions. But Satan will not be loosed to deceive all the nations until the end.

17
The New Jerusalem
(21:1–22:5)

The last vision, chapters 21–22, is of the New Heavens and New Earth and New Jerusalem. Coming as it does after the Millennium, we are inclined to take it as a picture of things after the Last Judgment, and I think 21:1–8 is just that: a picture of the everlasting kingdom after the last assize. But the New Jerusalem is also a millennial reality, because the gates of the city are open, converts are coming in, and the Spirit and Bride are evangelizing (21:24; 22:17).

What made the heavens and earth new was not something physical, but something governmental. The new heavens and earth came at the Ascension of Jesus to heaven, for now a Man was at last in heaven on the Throne with God, and at Pentecost, for the Spirit was at last released in full power to the earth. Also, Satan was cast out of heaven to the earth.

This was only the first stage, however. The fullness of the new heavens came when the saints joined Christ on the thrones in heaven; the fullness of the new earth came when Satan was removed from the earth.

But there is a progression in the manifestation of the new heavens and earth, because at the end, the heavenly sea will be removed. That sea was set up on the second day of creation as a temporary boundary between heaven and earth. After the last judgment it will be removed (21:1), and the New Jerusalem will take its place.

We have seen that the Bride had become formed by the time of the Battle of the Mountain of Festival Assembly (19:7–9). She was given white, holy garments then. Now we read that New Jerusalem is made ready as a Bride adorned for her Husband (21:2); she is given glorious, colored garments over her white, holy ones.

What does this mean? Wasn't the Church fully formed at Pentecost? No. The Church was *initially* formed in her New Creation fullness at Pentecost, but over the next 40 years there was still some Church-forming work to be done. It was the duty of the Apostles and Prophets of the Church to do this. First, they had to complete the Bible. Second, they had to weave Jew and God-fearing Gentile into one new body in Christ, a process that took some time and involved some difficulty, as the epistles of Paul show us. When the process was completed, that Firstfruits Church was privileged to join Her Lord outside the gates of Jerusalem in martyrdom (14:20). Then and only then was the Bride fully prepared and formed. The period of "to the Jew first" was over. The crucified and resurrected Jesus now has a martyred and resurrected Bride.

Now the Bride is ready, and the Marriage Feast begins. The Feast continues until the end of history, and then Bride and Groom are joined in the full experience of marital bliss (which, of course, comes after the feast).

When we turn to 21:9ff., however, we see aspects of the New Jerusalem that clearly do not apply to the everlasting kingdom, such as nations coming in through open doors. Thus, while the fullness of the New Jerusalem is future, she already existed from Pentecost forward (see Hebrews 12:22; Galatians 4:26). So, the New Jerusalem is a picture of the Church after Pentecost—and not only of the Church, but also of the discipled nations, who gradually come into her as the Great Commission is fulfilled over all the earth (21:24).

In the Bible, God builds His sanctuary out of the spoils of His defeated enemies who oppress His bride. The Tabernacle was built of the spoils of Egypt, and the Temple of the spoils of David's wars against the Philistines. The great visionary City-Temple of Ezekiel 40–48 (symbolizing the Restoration Covenant era) was built of the spoils of the war against Gog and Magog (Ezekiel 38–39; the book of Esther). Similarly, New Jerusalem is built of the spoils of Babylon, listed in 18:12–13.

The first two sanctuaries were really built: the Tabernacle and Solomon's Temple. The second two are too glorious to have a physical existence: Ezekiel's Restoration Temple and the New Jerusalem. Rather, they are literary Temple-Cities, which show Spiritual realities in the same way as the physical Tabernacle and Temple of earlier times did.

The New Jerusalem is a giant pyramid, a symbolic holy mountain, occupying the place where the firmament once was, whose top extends to the throne in heaven. It is guarded by a high wall, with servant messengers at the gates. (These "angels" are pastors, as in Revelation 2–3.) The city is built on the foundation stones of the twelve martyred apostles, with Jesus Christ as martyred Chief Cornerstone. The stones are the gemstones of the tribes of Israel, transfigured into the twelve apostles, while the pearly gates come from the Gentile sea, for this new fully-formed Church combines both former Jew and former Gentile into one new body.

The City is Temple and the Temple is City. This does not mean that the distinction between Church and State has disappeared, but that the Church is a microcosm of everything the State must be. The Church arrives before the converted nations, and disciples them, according to the Great Commission.

The poisonous waters of Wormwood are gone, and a stream of life-giving water, the Holy Spirit, flows from God's throne, bringing new life to all the world.

Finally, as the dead saints rule in heaven on the thrones of the archangels, so the living saints on earth reign forever and ever (22:5), discipling the world.

18

The Final Reminders

(22:6–21)

The visions are over. John is reminded to tell the seven churches that these events are shortly coming to pass. They will be tested and tried, but they can stand firm, knowing that Jesus will shortly vindicate them, even as He Himself is vindicated. If they (and we!) do not stand firm, then the contents of the now-opened Book will be visited on them (and us), just as it was on Babylon and the Beast. The sermon closes with a benediction (22:21).

For Further Reading

As noted in the Introduction, *The Vindication of Jesus Christ* is a summary of several years of studies and lectures. The complete lecture series on Revelation by James B. Jordan consists of 204 messages, 45–50 minutes in length, with an accompanying study guide of 450 pages. As one might expect, this lecture series spends time in various other parts of the Bible that form background to Revelation, especially Daniel, Zechariah, Ezekiel, and relevant New Testament passages. The list price for the entire series is $1000.00. The Revelation lectures can also be purchased in installments or downloaded from wordmp3.com.

For more information on this and on various papers and taped lectures on Revelation and related topics, write for a catalogue:

Biblical Horizons
P.O. Box 1096
Niceville, FL 32588

or visit us online at:

www.biblicalhorizons.com